# I Am Abel

Dorrance Publishing Co
585 Alpha Drive
Pittsburgh, PA 15238
Visit our website at *www.dorrancebookstore.com*

ISBN: 978-1-6491-3135-5
eISBN: 978-1-6491-3642-8

# I Am Abel

Deputy J. M. Froelich

**DORRANCE**
PUBLISHING CO
EST. 1920
PITTSBURGH, PENNSYLVANIA 15238

# I Am Abel

Deputy J. M. Froelich

**HI, MY NAME IS ABEL,** and I am a police K-9 working dog. You may have seen police K-9 dogs on TV or even in person. I am going to tell you how I became a police K-9 dog.

I was born on April 12, 2016, in Ontario, Canada, at Baden K-9, which is a special kennel where special puppies are born. All the puppies born there are raised to one day maybe become working dogs, like police dogs, military working dogs, rescue dogs, and security dogs. I am a Belgian Malinois (pronounced Mal-in-wah). When I was a real young puppy, I spent a lot of time with my mom and my brother. As I got to be older, the man who owned the kennel, Mr. Mike, and his son, Mr. Joshua, would come around and play with me and exercise me. The kennel was on a big farm, and there were many other dogs, cats, geese, cows, and other animals around. Sometimes people would come, and sometimes dogs would leave with these people, but I didn't know why.

One day, when I was 10 months old in February of 2017, a tall man came to the kennel, and Mr. Joshua brought him to see my brother and I. Mr. Joshua took my brother and I out to the field near the pond to play, and the man watched me run and jump. He watched my brother, too, but he seemed to really like watching me. I didn't know why he liked watching me so much, but I was having fun running and running and jumping and playing.

After a little while, the man talked to Mr. Joshua and then he left, and Mr. Joshua took me back to my dog house area. I didn't think I would ever see the tall man again, but then a month later on March 10, 2017, Mr. Mike came and got me real early one morning and took me on a leash to his house. I had never been to the house before. It was cold outside that day, and when he took me inside, I laid down in the warm dining room area.

A little later the tall man came in. I thought, *Hey I remember that guy.*

Mr. Mike talked to the man and then hooked a leash to my collar and handed the end of the leash to the man, and the man led me outside. I remember Mr. Mike saying, "Here is your new partner," to the tall man. I didn't even know what a partner was.

The man led me outside and over to his SUV. I was a little scared. I didn't know what was going on. The tall man bent down and stroked my head and said to me, "Well, buddy, we are going to be partners and work together. There is a lot you are going to have to learn, but I feel in my heart that you can do it. Your name is Abel. You are named after the very first Sheriff of Jefferson County, New York. His name was Abel Sherman. You are going to become a police K-9 dog, and together we are going to protect and serve the people of Jefferson County New York. My name is Deputy Jeff, and I am a Deputy Sheriff and K-9 Handler."

We then walked to a classroom building that was at the kennel on the farm. There, we met up with about 20 other dogs and their handlers. We spent a long day in class, and we did different simple things to get to know our handlers better. At the end of the class, Deputy Jeff put me in his car and took me to place called a motel. I had never been to one before. He took me inside the room at the motel and let me sniff around some. There were a lot of new smells I had never smelled before. Deputy Jeff then told me, "Be good for a few minutes, I am really dirty from training today and need a shower."

Deputy Jeff then disappeared into a smaller room, and I heard water running. Well, I didn't want to be alone so I ran into the room and jumped right into the thing that was shooting water at Deputy Jeff. I learned that that was a shower. Deputy Jeff laughed at me and said, "You are going to get all wet, Abel." Then he pushed me out of the shower thing, but I wanted to be with Deputy Jeff, so I jumped right back in. Well, I got wet alright, and Deputy Jeff just laughed and said, "Okay, goofy, you can stay, you could probably use a bath, too."

After that shower thing, Deputy Jeff put on some comfortable clothes and put some food in a bowl for me. I was so hungry, I ate all the food as fast as I could. It was really good. I then got a drink of water and looked for Deputy Jeff. He was laying on this thing called a bed, so I jumped up on it with him. It was really soft. I had never been on a bed before. He then turned on this box thing called a TV. I had never seen one before, and there were sounds and pictures coming from it, and I was a little nervous of it at first, but I got used to it.

Deputy Jeff got out this round thing called a ball and threw it on the floor, and it bounced all over the place. I jumped off the bed and went and sniffed the ball thing, but I wasn't really interested in it. Deputy Jeff picked it up and tossed it over and over again, but I really wasn't interested in that ball thing.

Deputy Jeff said, "Hmmm…you don't like balls, huh? I have to find something you like to play with because we have to have a reward for you when you do your job well."

I didn't know what a reward was. Then Deputy Jeff pulled this thing out that had two handles on it. He called it a tug toy and asked me if I liked to play tug. I didn't know what tug was, but Deputy Jeff showed me the tug toy, and I sniffed at it, and then I bit down on it. Deputy Jeff started pulling on in, so I bit harder and pulled back as hard as I could. I started shaking my head and pulling and pulling. I thought, *Wow, this is really fun!*

Then Deputy Jeff let go of the tug toy. I was like, *Why did he do that I was having fun?*

So, I tried to shove the toy back into his hand, so he would play some more. This tug stuff was fun. Deputy Jeff laughed and said, "Well, we know what you like, Abel, you like to play tug of war, so let's play!" and he grabbed the tug toy.

We played tug, and he would let go after a while, and I would be like, *Wooo Hoo! I win, let's do it again!* and I would try and shove the tug toy back into his hand, and he would grab it, and we would tug again and again. I was having so much fun.

After a few more rounds of tug of war, Deputy Jeff said, "Well, partner, we are going to need to get some rest. We have class again tomorrow."

So, I curled up next to him on that soft bed thing. I put my head on Deputy Jeff, and I thought, *It's so comfortable and warm here.* I fell asleep with my head on Deputy Jeff's chest, listening to his heartbeat. I thought, *I like Deputy Jeff, and I hope I stay with him.*

In the morning, we went back to the class, and we did this for two more days. Then we got into Deputy Jeff's car, and he told me we had a long drive ahead of us. We drove for a long time, almost six hours, and then we stopped at where he works in New York. Deputy Jeff told me that this was the Jefferson County Sheriff's Office, and this was where we would go to work. We then got into another car. This one seemed special. It was black and had words on the side that said, "Sheriff K-9 Unit." I was still trying to figure out what this K-9 thing was. The car had lights on top of the roof, and there was a special place for me to ride in too, right behind Deputy Jeff. We then drove to what Deputy Jeff said was his home. We got out, and he let me run around in the yard. There was what I thought was a really big pond like at the kennel where I was born in his back yard, but it turned out to be a big lake called Lake Ontario. I also met his wife and son, who I would be living with. They were really nice and seemed to be happy I was going to live with them.

*K-9 Abel and K-9 Bruin doing obedience training*

For the next few months, I rode around with Deputy Jeff in his Sheriff's K-9 patrol car, getting used to the sights and sounds of being a police dog. Then one day, Deputy Jeff said, "Tomorrow, we are going away for a few months." He told me we were going to start school at the New York State Police K-9 Academy in Cooperstown New York.

The next morning, we left and drove to the academy. At the academy, I met my new classmates. There were 12 dogs and their handlers in my class. I made some new dog friends. There was K-9 Jada, K-9 Theo, K-9 Nala, K-9 Artie, K-9 Matty, and more. I also met my teachers. There was Lieutenant Jay, Sergeant Doug,

*K-9 Abel and K-9 Schini train together*

7

*K-9 Abel learns to jump obstacles*

*K-9 Abel learns to go through tunnels*

*K-9 Abel doing special training in smoke*

Trooper Ryan, and Trooper Tony. For the next three months, every Monday through Friday from 8 a.m. until about 4:30 p.m., I had training classes. I had to learn so much. I had to learn how to jump through windows, jump over tall fences, climb really high stairs, go through dark tunnels, and jump or climb over lots of tough obstacles.

I had to learn to use my nose to sniff out illegal drugs. I had to learn to search for bad guys in a building. I had to learn a lot of obedience commands like sit, lay down, come, stay, jump, and more. I had to learn to track for bad guys who ran away and to track for people who got lost like in the woods. I had to learn how to catch and apprehend a bad guy and how to protect my partner, Deputy Jeff.

It was at the K-9 Academy that I learned what the word partner meant. It meant that Deputy Jeff and I were a team. We would always be together, and I liked that. We would be together at work and at home. All of the dogs in my class did a great job, and we all learned what we needed to learn. We all became what is called "dual purpose" police K-9 dogs. That means we could all catch bad guys, track people, search buildings, and protect our handlers. Some of us learned to sniff out drugs, and the others learned to sniff out bombs and explosives. We trained and trained and trained. I loved my school. I loved training and learning stuff every day. Whenever I found the drugs I was sniffing for or found

*K-9 Abel playing fetch*

the bad guy or did my obedience real well, Deputy Jeff would pull out the tug toy and play and play with me. This made me want to do the best I could at everything because I sure love playing with Deputy Jeff.

On the weekends, we would go home, and I could relax a little bit. I would go swimming in the big lake and play fetch and just be a dog. I bet some of you have dogs at home, too, and you play with them. Who has a dog at home, or a cat, or other pet that they like to play with?

One day at the academy, Deputy Jeff came to me and said, "Tomorrow we start certifying on everything you learned here." He explained to me that certifying meant that I had to take a test on everything I learned at the academy, and if I passed everything, I would become a certified K-9 police dog. Certifying meant that I would get a certificate, which is like a diploma that you get when you graduate from school. If I got certified, I would graduate from the New York State Police K-9 Academy and be a real police K-9 dog.

The next day, we started the tests, and the tests lasted about three days, and when it was over, I had done really, really well. I passed everything on my first try, and Deputy Jeff was so proud of me. When I finished, he grabbed me in his arms and gave me lots of scratches and belly rubs, and he got out the tug toy, and we played and played.

The next morning was graduation day, and we got our certificates and said goodbye to the other handlers and my dog friends. We then went home. We had a few days off and then we went to work at the Sheriff's Office. On our first night at work, a local TV crew came and interviewed Deputy Jeff and I, and I got to be on TV. Then we got into Deputy Jeff's patrol car and went out on patrol. Now I was a certified police K-9, and I had a job to do.

Whenever Deputy Jeff and I are needed, we go search for illegal drugs, which are really bad for you. We go search for bad guys, search for lost people, and work to protect and assist the other deputies, state troopers, and police officers who work in our

*K-9 Abel on graduation day from the New York State Police K-9 Academy*

*Graduation day*

county. Twice every month, I have to go to training to practice my skills. It is kind of like if you have ever played a sport or played a musical instrument, you have to practice right? Me too. Practicing makes me better at my job as a K-9. Every year I have to re-certify, too, to show that I can still do my job. I also got certified from the New York Department of Criminal Justice Services and national certification from the North American Police Work Dog Association. Deputy Jeff says I am a very special dog to have all those certifications, but I don't care about all the certificates. I just like to do my job and play with Deputy Jeff.

*K-9 Abel card*

**Breed :** Belgian Malinois
**D.O.B. :** 4/12/16 Ontario, Canada
**Shield # :** 55
**Handler :** Deputy J.M. Froelich

K-9 Abel is a dual purpose K-9, trained and certified in advance narcotics detection, obedience, building searches, suspect apprehension, and handler protection. He joined the Jefferson County Sheriff's Office on March 12, 2017.

*Safety Tip: Always wear a properly fitted life vest when out on a boat. K-9 Abel wears his!*

JEFFERSON COUNTY SHERIFF'S OFFICE
753 Waterman Drive Watertown, NY 13601
(315) 788-1441

www.customK9cards.com

Work is real exciting, and I can't wait to get into my patrol car and go to work. I now know what it means to be a police K-9, and I am very proud to be a Deputy Sheriff K-9. They even gave me my own badge. My badge number is 55.

When it comes to being a K-9, I am always ready, willing, and able, because…

I AM K-9 ABEL!

*K-9 Abel and his special patrol car*

*K-9 Abel in the Jefferson County Fair parade*

Explain before the book is read that there will be a fun quiz at the end, and everyone needs to pay attention. Teachers, here are some questions to help the kids understand what was read:

1) Where was Abel born?
2) What kind of dog is Abel?
3) How long was Abel training at the academy?
4) What is Abel's favorite toy?
5) What is something Abel is trained to do?
6) Who was Abel named after?

**ANSWERS**

1) Baden K-9; or Ontario; or Canada 2) Belgian Malinois 3) Three months 4) Tug toy 5) Tracking; searching for and catching bad guys or lost people; sniffing for drugs; obedience; and protecting Deputy Jeff 6) Abel Sherman; or the first Sheriff of Jefferson County New York

*K-9 Abel on the Protecting K-9 Heroes logo*

*The author would like to thank:*
The Jefferson County Sheriff's Office for
allowing me to be a K-9 Handler;
The North Country Kennel Club for their
support of our K-9 unit;
Baden K-9 Ontario, Canada, for K-9 Abel himself,
my partner, my protector, and my friend; and
The New York State Police K-9 Academy
for assisting in the training of K-9 Abel.

For more information on how you can help
K-9 working dogs, please go online and visit
protectingk9heroes.com

Proceeds from the sale of this book go to providing
first aid kits and protective gear for K-9 teams.

I Am Abel

Deputy J. M. Froelich

This book is dedicated to all K-9 Handlers the world over.
No humans share a stronger bond with a dog than we do.
Stay safe.